More WORDS and PICTURES

Compiled by Colin Clark
Illustrations by Terry Burton

balloons

robot

birthday card

fizzy drinks

sandwich

magician

straws

paper chain

presents

cake

biscuit

invitation

yo-yo

party hat

jelly

xylophone

Brown Watson
ENGLAND

Wild Animals

hippopotamus (hippo)

panda

elephant

kangaroo

koala

dolphin

swordfish

giraffe

parrot

gorilla

peacock

wolf

walrus

lizard

hedgehog

lion

armadillo

leopard

swan

rhinoceros (rhino)

crocodile

zebra

platypus

whale

shark

octopus

bat

ostrich

camel

polar bear

monkey

tiger

seal

skunk

reindeer

badger

owl

cobra (a snake)

3

People at Work

pilot

cook

firefighter

soldier

mechanic

gardener

bus driver

teacher

baker

builder

plumber

librarian

shop-assistant

painter and decorator

vet

TV presenter

photographer

wrestler

cowboy

window-cleaner

postman

model

dancer

musician

police officer

sailor

air stewardess

woodworker

electrician

hairdresser

banker

clown

waiter

miner

tailor

judge

opera singer

At the Doctor

torch

syringe

stethoscope

receptionist

bottle of medicine

couch

rubber hammer

doctor

prescription

medical books

height gauge

bottle of pills

eye chart

first-aid box

bandage

measuring beaker

filing cabinet

scales

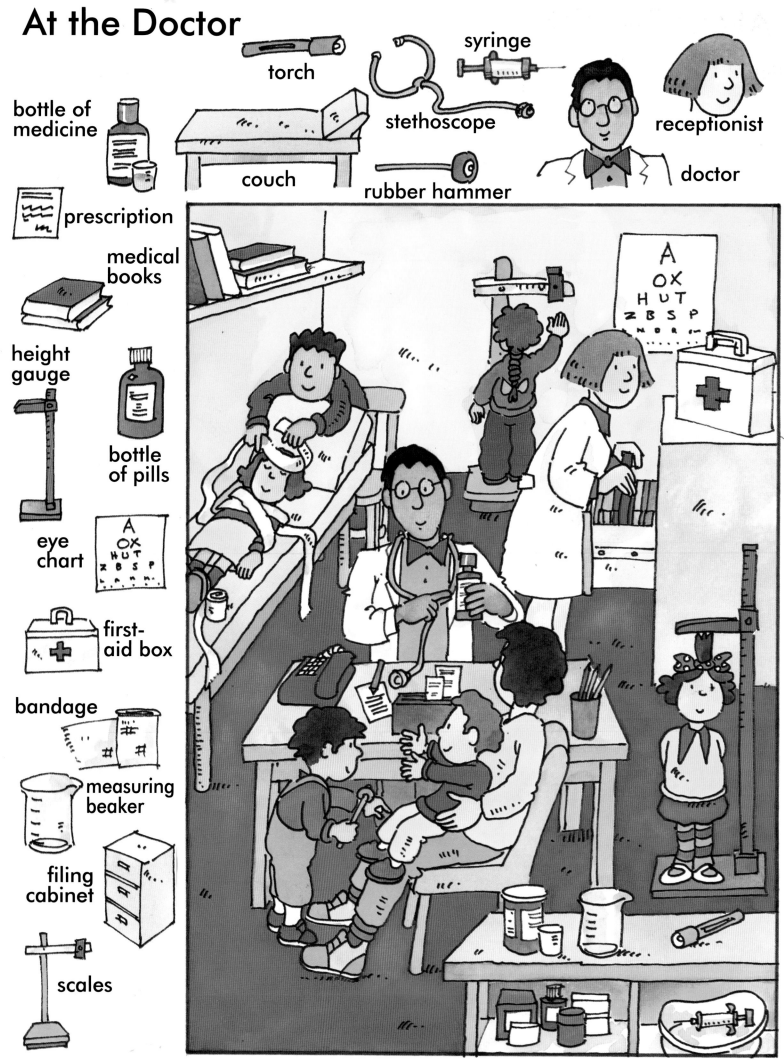

6

At the Dentist

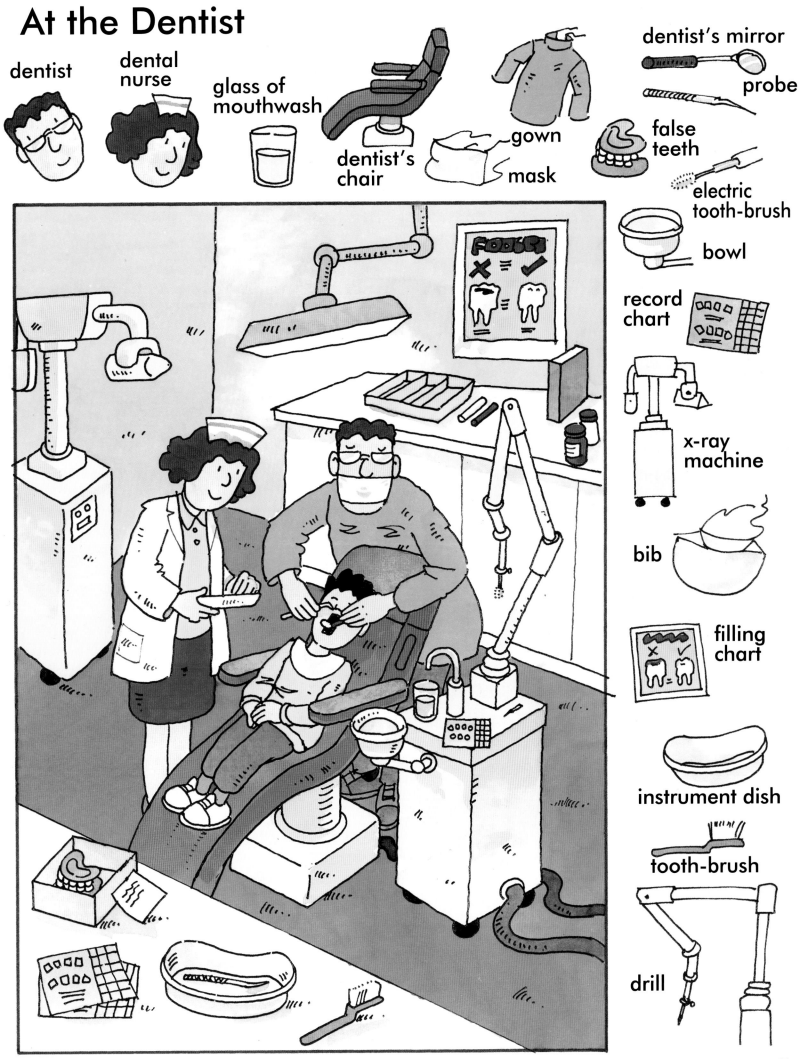

dentist

dental nurse

glass of mouthwash

dentist's chair

gown

mask

dentist's mirror

probe

false teeth

electric tooth-brush

bowl

record chart

x-ray machine

bib

filling chart

instrument dish

tooth-brush

drill

Games and Sports

diving-board

darts

tennis

football

ice skating

diving

skiing

baseball

golf

show-jumping

judo

cycling

leap-frog

American football

table tennis

rowing

marbles

archery

swimming

target

chess

ice hockey

cards

computer game

rugby

cricket

sailing

blind-man's buff

dressing-up

gymnastics

running

tug of war

riding

snooker

board game

9

Partytime

busy grown-up

robot

thank-you kiss

lots of crumbs

jam doughnuts

yo-yo

broken toy

sparklers

fizzy drinks

birthday cards

HAPPY BIRTH DAY

sticky toffees

sandwich

balloons

candles

iced cake

drinking straws

PETE

JOHN PAT

paper hat

biscuit

magician's hat

cloak

cracker

magician

party invitation

jack-in-the-box

paper chain

crying child

jelly

nervous cat

xylophone

name tags

PAT

JOHN

tablecloth

presents

In Storybooks

ghost

dragon

knight in armour

Santa

sleigh

sack of toys

reindeer

turret

castle

unicorn

crown

giant

drawbridge

moat

throne

lovely princess

queen

page-boy

spinning-wheel

mermaid

12

witch

witch's cauldron

broomstick

wizard

magic wand

magic carpet

skull and crossbones (flag)

flying horse

buried treasure

pirate

handsome prince

fairy

palace

wishing-well

king

seven dwarfs

13

Words in Action

a writer writing

a painter painting

standing up

lying down

kneeling

eating ice-cream

laughing

sneezing

watching T.V.

hiding

brushing the dog

throwing

hurrying

digging a hole

chopping wood

sewing

making

blowing a trumpet

14

marching

falling over

sitting down

a singer singing

a reader reading

drinking lemonade

crying

crawling

listening to the radio

saluting

catching

sweeping the floor

knitting

jumping

combing your hair

finding

cutting the grass

15

Builders and Buildings

block of flats

hotel

theatre

crane

building site

bricks

hod

dump truck

safety helmet

scaffolding

bulldozer

cement mixer

navvy

bricklayer

factory

snack bar

terraced house

multi-storey car park

sports pavilion

cottage

tennis court

power station

16

office block

hospital

stately home

synagogue

church

police station

wooden hut

cinema

pub

school

restaurant

park

playground

mosque

17

On the Water

oil tanker

buoy

bow

stern

cruise liner

diving bell

speedboat

houseboat

barge

hydrofoil

paddle-steamer

ferry-boat

tug-boat

hover craft

submarine

mast

sail

yacht

In the Garage

car transporter

spanner

windscreen wipers

headlights

wing mirror

tyre

bumper

boot

exhaust pipe

foot-pump

roof-rack

car-wash

trailer

mechanic

tyre lever

jack

oil leak

battery

19

At the Railway Station

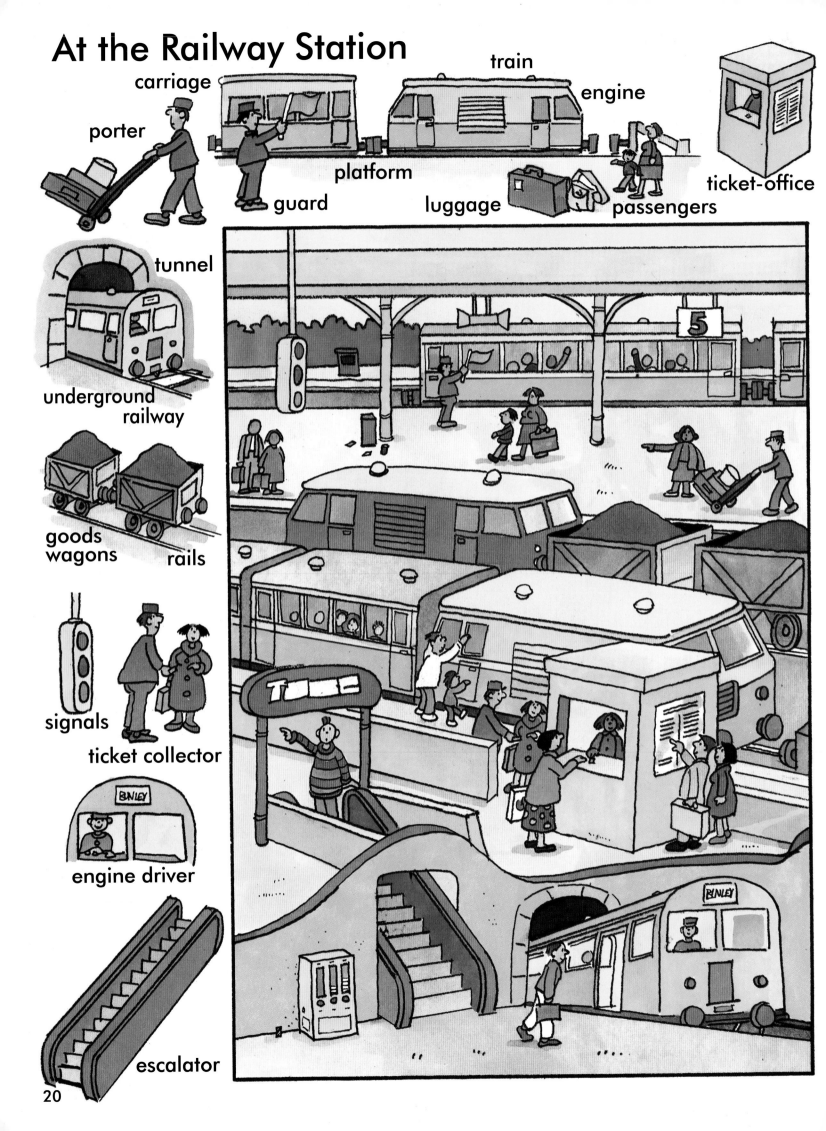

carriage

porter

train

engine

platform

guard

luggage

passengers

ticket-office

tunnel

underground railway

goods wagons

rails

signals

ticket collector

engine driver

escalator

20

At the Airport

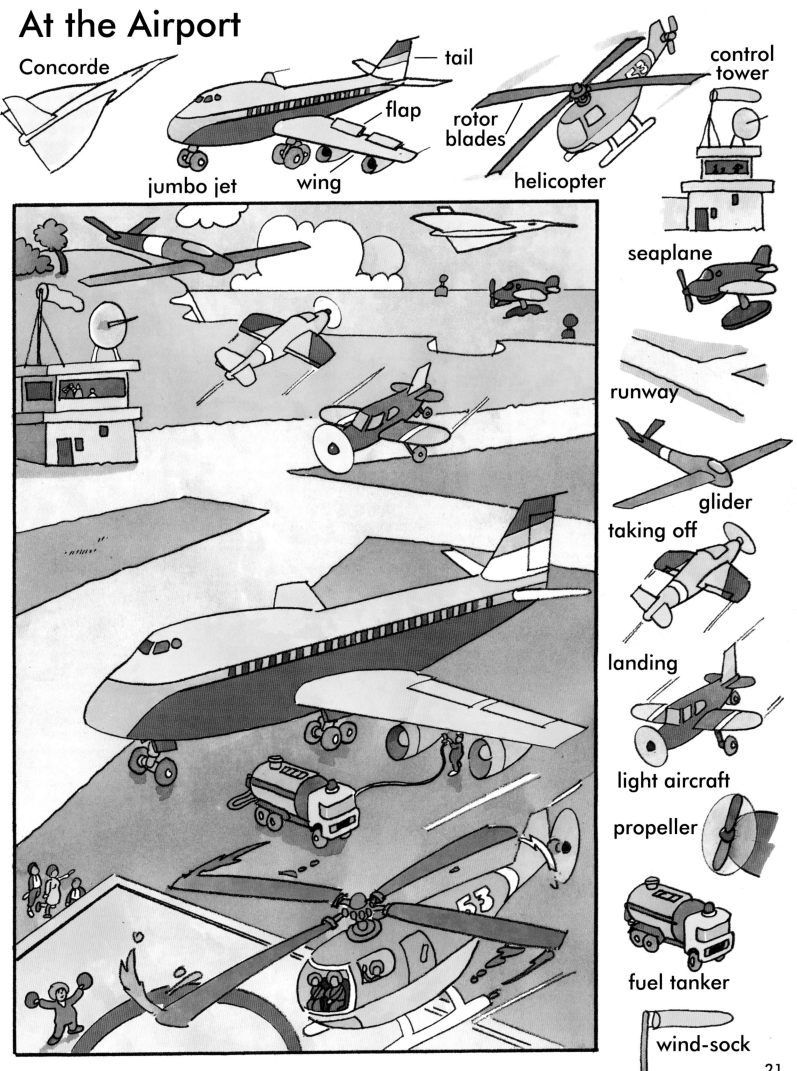

Concorde

jumbo jet

tail

flap

wing

rotor blades

helicopter

control tower

seaplane

runway

glider

taking off

landing

light aircraft

propeller

fuel tanker

wind-sock

At the Seaside

splashing

crab

lighthouse

flippers

swimsuit

parasol

boatman

deckchair

seaweed

starfish

motor-boat

wind-surfer

rubber ring

sand-castle

inflatable boat

seagull

beach-mat

chain

anchor

22

fishing-boat

paddle

waves

beach

snorkel

pool

seashells

sunhat

sea-wall

beach-ball

jellyfish

water-skiier

surfboard

pump

bollard

flag

All about Plants

parts of a tree

twig

branch

leaf

bark

falling leaf

trunk

sapling

roots

fallen leaves

oak tree

fir tree

palm tree

monkey-puzzle tree

what grows on trees?

pineapple

banana

coconut

pine cone

apple

chestnut

mulberry

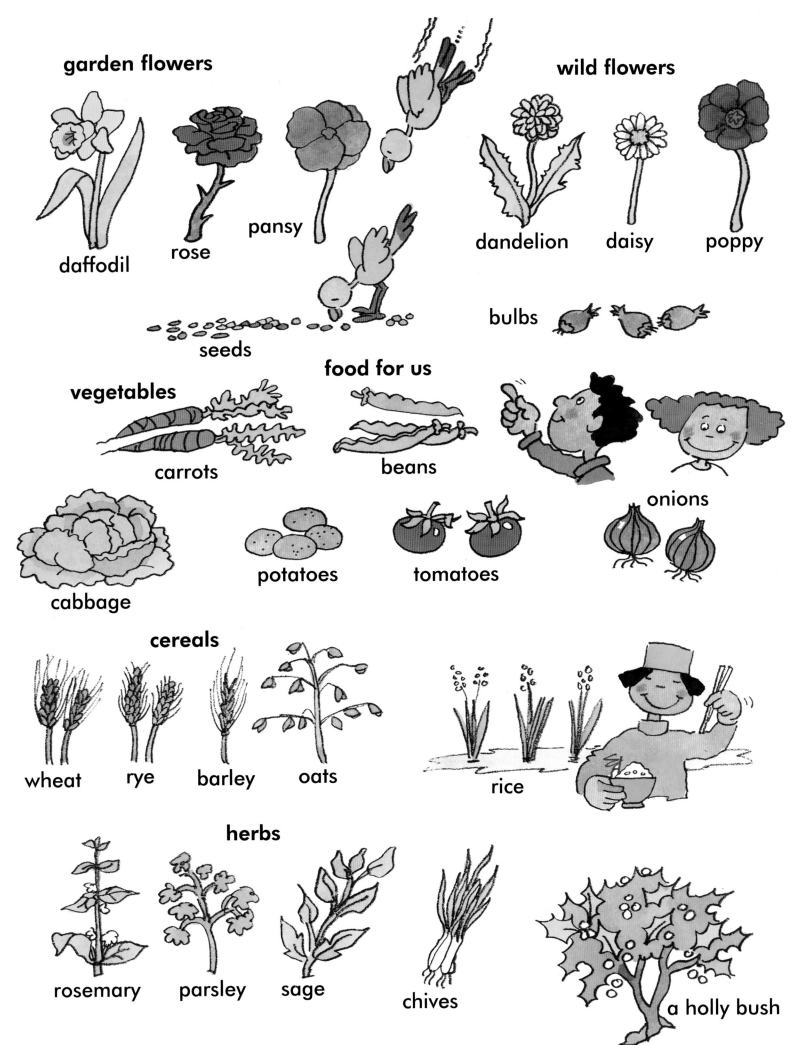

garden flowers

daffodil

rose

pansy

wild flowers

dandelion

daisy

poppy

seeds

bulbs

food for us

vegetables

carrots

beans

onions

cabbage

potatoes

tomatoes

cereals

wheat

rye

barley

oats

rice

herbs

rosemary

parsley

sage

chives

a holly bush

Opposites

fat

dirty

thin

clean

wet

dry

big

sad

happy

small

good

bad

tidy

untidy

easy

difficult

fast

slow

26

Where are they?

in

out

up

above

below

first

last

high

low

over

under

behind

between

in front

left

right

down

far

near

Colours and Numbers

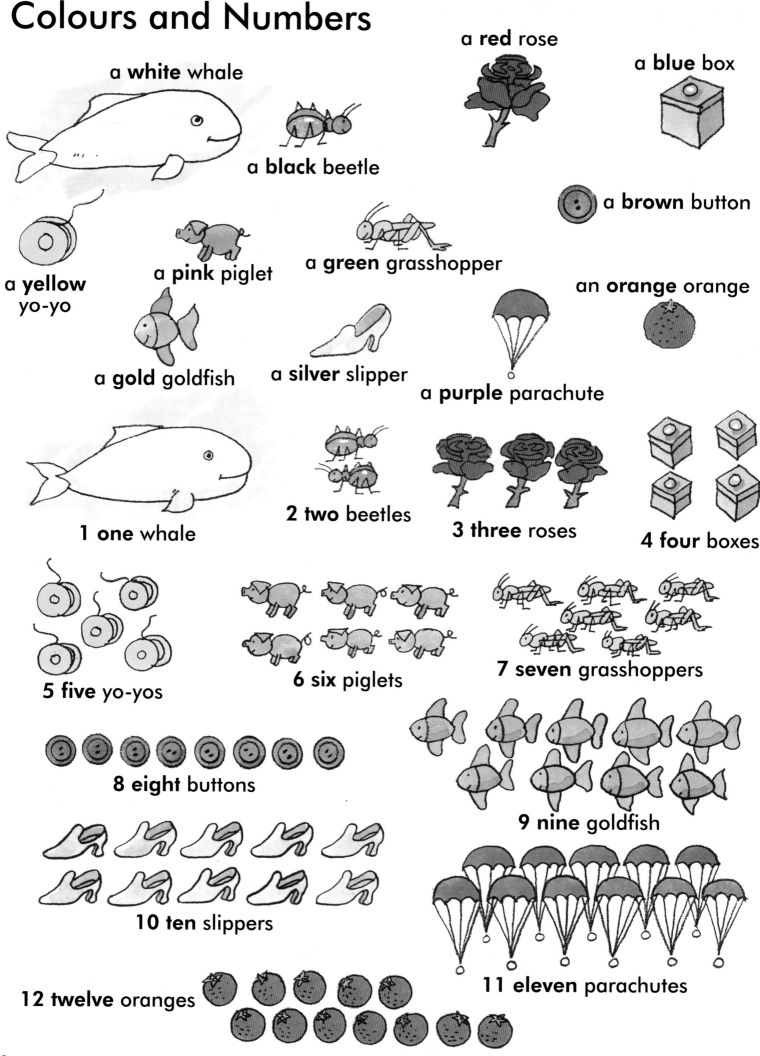

a **white** whale

a **black** beetle

a **red** rose

a **blue** box

a **brown** button

a **yellow** yo-yo

a **pink** piglet

a **green** grasshopper

an **orange** orange

a **gold** goldfish

a **silver** slipper

a **purple** parachute

1 one whale

2 two beetles

3 three roses

4 four boxes

5 five yo-yos

6 six piglets

7 seven grasshoppers

8 eight buttons

9 nine goldfish

10 ten slippers

11 eleven parachutes

12 twelve oranges

Shapes and Comparisons

a square

a circle

an oval

a cube

a cone

a triangle

a star

a crescent

a diamond

a corner

a point

a straight line

a curved line

a toad

a bigger toad

the biggest toad

a long tail

a longer tail

the longest tail

little

less

the least

some

more

the most

a few sweets

fewer sweets

the fewest sweets

a giraffe

a taller giraffe

the tallest giraffe

Words in this Book

above	27	cabbage	25	doctor	6	gown	7
action	14	cabinet, filing	6	dog, brushing	14	grass, cutting	15
air stewardess	5	cake, iced	10	dolphin	2	grasshopper	28
aircraft, light	21	camel	3	down	27	green	28
airport	21	candles	10	dragon	12	grown-up	10
American football	8	car-wash	19	drawbridge	12	grows	24
anchor	22	car park	16	dressing-up	9	guard	20
animals, wild	2	car transporter	19	drill	7	gymnastics	9
apple	24	cards	9	drinking lemonade	15	hair, combing	15
archery	9	carpet, magic	13	drinking straws	10	hairdresser	5
armadillo	2	carriage	20	drinks, fizzy	10	hammer, rubber	6
armour, knight in	12	carrots	25	driver, engine	20	handsome prince	13
bad	26	castle	12	dry	26	happy	26
badger	3	cat, nervous	11	dump truck	16	hat, magician's	11
baker	4	catching	15	dwarfs	13	hat, paper	11
balloons	10	cauldron, witch's	13	easy	26	headlights	19
banana	24	cement mixer	16	eating ice-cream	14	hedgehog	2
bandage	6	cereals	25	eight	28	height gauge	6
banker	5	chain	22	electric tooth-brush	7	helicopter	21
bar, snack	16	chain, paper	11	electrician	5	helmet, safety	16
barge	18	chess	9	elephant	2	hiding	14
bark	24	chestnut	24	eleven	28	high	27
barley	25	child, crying	11	engine	20	hippopotamus (hippo)	2
baseball	8	chives	25	engine driver	20	hod	16
bat	3	chopping wood	14	escalator	20	hole, digging	14
battery	19	church	17	exhaust pipe	19	holly bush	25
beach	23	cinema	17	eye chart	6	home, stately	17
beach-ball	23	circle	29	factory	16	horse, flying	13
beach-mat	22	clean	26	fairy	13	hospital	17
beaker, measuring	6	cloak	11	fallen leaves	24	hotel	16
beans	25	clown	5	falling leaf	24	house, terraced	16
beetle	28	cobra	3	falling over	15	houseboat	18
behind	27	coconut	24	false teeth	7	hovercraft	18
bell, diving	18	colours	28	far	27	hurrying	14
below	27	combing hair	15	fast	26	hut, wooden	17
between	27	comparisons	29	fat	26	hydrofoil	18
big	7	computer game	9	ferry-boat	18	ice-cream, eating	14
big	26	collector, ticket	20	few	29	ice hockey	9
bigger	29	Concorde	21	fewer	29	ice skating	8
biggest	29	cone	29	fewest	29	iced cake	10
birthday cards	10	cone, pine	24	filing cabinet	6	in	27
biscuit	11	control tower	21	filling chart	7	in front	27
black	28	cook	4	finding	15	inflatable boat	22
blades, motor	21	corner	29	fir tree	24	instrument dish	7
blind-man's buff	9	cottage	16	fire fighter	4	invitation, party	11
block of flats	16	couch	6	first	27	jack	19
block, office	17	court, tennis	16	first-aid box	6	jack-in-the-box	11
blowing a trumpet	14	cowboy	4	fishing-boat	23	jam doughnuts	10
blue	28	crab	22	five	28	jelly	11
board game	9	cracker	11	fizzy drinks	10	jellyfish	23
boat, inflatable	22	crane	16	flag	13, 23	jet, jumbo	21
boatman	22	crawling	15	flap	21	judge	5
bollard	23	crescent	29	flats, block of	16	judo	8
books, medical	6	cricket	9	flippers	22	jumbo jet	21
boot	19	crocodile	3	floor, sweeping	15	jumping	15
bottle of medicine	6	crown	12	flowers, garden	25	kangaroo	2
bottle of pills	6	cruise liner	18	flowers, wild	25	king	13
bow	18	crying	15	flying horse	13	kiss, thank-you	10
bowl	7	crying child	11	food	25	koala	2
box	28	cube	29	foot-pump	19	kneeling	14
box, first-aid	6	curved	29	football	8	knight in armour	12
branch	24	cutting grass	15	football, American	8	knitting	15
bricklayer	16	cycling	8	four	28	landing	21
bricks	16	daffodil	25	front	27	last	27
broken toy	10	daisy	25	fuel tanker	21	laughing	14
broomstick	13	dancer	5	game, board	9	leaf, leaves	24
brown	28	dandelion	25	game, computer	9	leak, oil	19
brushing the dog	14	darts	8	games	8	leap-frog	8
builder	4	deckchair	22	garden flowers	25	least	29
builders	16	decorator	4	gardener	4	left	27
building site	16	dental nurse	7	ghost	12	lemonade, drinking	15
buildings	16	dentist	7	giant	12	leopard	2
bulbs	25	dentist's chair	7	giraffe	20, 29	less	29
bulldozer	16	dentist's mirror	7	glass of mouthwash	7	lever, tyre	19
bumper	19	diamond	29	glider	21	librarian	4
buoy	18	difficult	26	gold	28	light aircraft	21
buried treasure	13	digging a hole	14	goldfish	28	lighthouse	22
bus driver	4	dirty	26	golf	8	line	29
bush, holly	25	diving	8	good	26	liner, cruise	18
busy grown-up	10	diving bell	18	goods wagons	20	lion	2
button	28	diving-board	8	gorilla	2	listening to the radio	15

little	29	piglet	28
lizard	2	pills	6
long	29	pilot	4
longer	29	pine cone	24
longest	29	pineapple	24
lots of crumbs	10	pink	28
lovely princess	12	pipe, exhaust	28
low	27	pirate	13
luggage	20	plants	24
lying down	14	platform	20
machine, x-ray	7	platypus	3
magic carpet	13	playground	17
magic wand	13	plumber	4
magician	11	point	29
magician's hat	11	polar bear	3
making	14	police officer	5
marbles	8	police station	17
marching	15	pool	23
mask	7	poppy	25
mast	18	porter	20
measuring beaker	6	postman	5
mechanic	4, 19	potatoes	25
medicine	6	power station	16
mermaid	12	prescription	6
miner	5	presents	11
mirror, wing	19	prince, handsome	13
mixer, cement	16	princess, lovely	12
moat	12	probe	7
model	5	propeller	21
monkey-puzzle tree	24	pub	17
more	29	pump	23
mosque	17	purple	28
most	29	queen	12
motor-boat	22	radio, listening	15
mulberry	24	rails	20
multistory car park	17	railway station	20
musician	5	railway, underground	20
name tags	11	reader	15
navvy	16	reading	15
near	27	receptionist	6
nervous cat	11	record chart	7
nine	28	red	28
numbers	28	reindeer	3, 12
nurse, dental	7	restaurant	17
oak tree	24	rhinoceros (rhino)	3
oats	25	rice	25
octopus	3	riding	9
office block	17	right	27
oil leak	19	robot	10
oil tanker	18	roof-rack	19
one	28	roots	24
onions	25	rose	25, 28
opera singer	5	rosemary	25
opposites	26	rotor, blades	21
orange	28	rowing	8
ostrich	3	rubber hammer	6
out	27	rubber ring	22
oval	29	rugby	9
over	27	running	9
owl	3	runway	21
paddle	23	rye	25
paddle-steamer	18	sack of toys	12
page-boy	12	sad	26
painter	4, 14	safety helmet	16
painting	14	sage	25
palace	13	sail	18
palm tree	24	sailing	9
panda	2	sailor	5
pansy	25	saluting	15
paper chain	11	sand-castle	22
paper hat	11	sandwich	10
parachute	28	Santa	12
parasol	22	sapling	24
park	17	scaffolding	16
parrot	2	scales	6
parsley	25	school	17
parts of a tree	24	sea-wall	23
party invitation	11	seagull	22
passengers	20	seal	3
pavilion, sports	16	seaplane	21
peacock	2	seashells	23
people	4	seaside	22
photographer	4	seaweed	22

seeds	25	throwing	14
seven	28	ticket collector	20
seven dwarfs	13	ticket-office	20
sewing	14	tidy	26
shapes	29	tiger	3
shark	3	toad	29
shop-assistant	4	toffees, sticky	10
show-jumping	8	tomatoes	25
signals	20	tooth-brush	7
silver	28	tooth-brush, electric	7
singer	15	torch	6
singer, opera	5	tower, control	21
singing	15	toy, broken	10
sitting down	15	toys, sack of	12
six	28	trailer	19
skating, ice	8	train	20
skiing	8	transporter, car	19
skull and crossbones	13	treasure, buried	13
skunk	3	tree	24
sleigh	12	tree, fir	24
slipper	28	tree, monkey-puzzle	24
slow	26	tree, oak	24
small	26	tree, palm	24
snack bar	16	triangle	29
snake	3	truck, dump	16
sneezing	14	trumpet, blowing	14
snooker	9	trunk	24
snorkel	23	tug-boat	18
soldier	4	tug-of-war	9
some	29	tunnel	20
spanner	19	turret	12
sparklers	10	TV, watching	14
speedboat	18	TV presenter	4
spinning-wheel	12	twelve	28
splashing	22	twig	24
sports	8	two	28
sports pavilion	16	tyre	19
square	29	tyre lever	19
standing up	14	under	27
star	29	underground railway	20
starfish	22	unicorn	12
stately home	17	untidy	26
station, police	17	up	27
station, power	16	us	25
station, railway	20	vegetables	25
stern	18	vet	4
stethoscope	6	wagons, goods	20
sticky toffees	10	waiter	5
storybooks	12	walrus	2
straight	29	wand, magic	13
straws, drinking	10	watching TV	14
submarine	18	water-skier	23
sunhat	23	waves	23
surfboard	23	wet	26
swan	2	whale	3, 28
sweeping the floor	15	wheat	25
swimming	9	where	27
swimsuit	22	white	28
swordfish	2	wild animals	2
synagogue	17	wild flowers	25
syringe	6	wind-sock	21
table tennis	8	wind-surfer	22
tablecloth	11	window-cleaner	5
tags, name	11	windscreen wipers	19
tail	21, 29	wing	21
tailor	5	wing mirror	19
taking off	21	wishing-well	13
taller	29	witch	13
tallest	29	witch's cauldron	13
tanker, fuel	21	wizard	13
tanker, oil	18	wolf	2
target	9	wood, chopping	14
teacher	4	wooden hut	17
teeth, false	7	woodworker	5
ten	28	words	14
tennis	8	work	4
tennis court	16	wrestler	4
terraced house	16	writer	14
thank-you kiss	10	writing	14
theatre	16	x-ray machine	7
thin	26	xylophone	11
three	28	yacht	18
throne	12	yellow	28
		yo-yo	10, 28
		zebra	3

Contents

Page

2	Wild Animals
4	People at Work
6	At the Doctor
7	At the Dentist
8	Games and Sports
10	Partytime
12	In Storybooks
14	Words in Action
16	Builders and Buildings
18	On the Water
19	In the Garage
20	At the Railway Station
21	At the Airport
22	At the Seaside
24	All about Plants
26	Opposites
27	Where are they?
28	Colours and Numbers
29	Shapes and Comparisons
30	Words in this Book

First published 1994 by Brown Watson, The Old Mill, 76 Fleckney Road, Kibworth Beauchamp, Leics, England

© 1994 Brown Watson

ISBN 0 7097 0963 3

Printed in Germany